Bibliographic information published by the German National Library:

The German National Library lists this publication in the National Bibliography; detailed bibliographic data are available on the Internet at http://dnb.dnb.de .

Imprint:

Copyright © 2010 GRIN Verlag
Print and binding: Books on Demand GmbH, Norderstedt Germany
ISBN: 9783668620773

This book at GRIN:

https://www.grin.com/document/388103

Lina Kudriavcevaite

"Cop Culture". The Main Aspects and Critiques

GRIN Verlag

GRIN - Your knowledge has value

Since its foundation in 1998, GRIN has specialized in publishing academic texts by students, college teachers and other academics as e-book and printed book. The website www.grin.com is an ideal platform for presenting term papers, final papers, scientific essays, dissertations and specialist books.

Visit us on the internet:

http://www.grin.com/

http://www.facebook.com/grincom

http://www.twitter.com/grin_com

The principal features and characteristics associated with 'cop culture' and the main recent critiques of the previous scholarly accounts of this concept

The notion of 'police culture' has been widely applied to understand the inner world of the police; it refers to a set of shared informal norms, beliefs and values, which underpins and informs police outlooks and behaviour towards people (Loftus, 2008). Social tendencies, whenever visible or not, are embodied in police practices, and thus are reflected in the 'cop culture'. It has been long speculated on causes, application, and outcomes of the police occupational culture by various researchers. As unfolded by Paoline (2003), most connotations of police culture are negative: it is seen as a barrier to reforming the police; it is also interpreted as a factor which endorses the violations of citizen's rights and misuses of police authority. Nonetheless, the collectiveness of culture has positive effects, for it helps to overcome the difficulties in everyday work. The culture can be used as a tool in learning the craft of policing. Moreover, police culture could be employed for regulating and preventing inappropriate police conduct, and gradually for reforming the police (Paoline, 2003).

The terms police culture(s), cop and canteen culture have entered the discourse of police studies. As Skolnick (in Westmarland, 2008) has unfolded, police behaviour is influenced by the underlying values and politics of the community that finances the police department. Recent studies on police culture phenomenon have recognized its potential for change and diversity; studies also discovered individual and organizational variations, and new challenges. Considering these variations, it would be more accurate to use a plural form when referring to the police culture, for a unified singular culture as such does not exist (Westmarland, 2008). However, some common persistent features, expressed throughout several decades, can be identified within police institutions. Skolnick (2009) emphasizes that representatives of various professions tend to share occupational features: they develop distinctive ways of perceiving and responding to their environment. As police officers are involved in offenders' apprehension, it might contribute to the professional suspiciousness, biases and prejudices. Indeed, even the training of police officers indicates the necessity for suspiciousness, because some events or physical surroundings may signal the likelihood of danger in advance (Skolnick, 2009).

As it is unfolded by several authors (in Reiner, 2010), there is a significant correlation between social and criminal injustice. Following theoretical rhetoric, individuals should be treated equally, due process rights must apply to all, and biased, subjective perspectives should be eliminated. Yet research demonstrates that the majority of people detained at police stations were drawn from the economically and socially marginal groups (Sanders, 1995). Increased negative attention to ethnic minority groups tends to have an impact on further social alienation. Under the controversial section 44 of anti-terrorism powers (Terrorism Act 2000) and section 60 powers of the Criminal Justice and Public Order Act (1994) – the powers that do not require a reasonable suspicion, – tens of thousands of people have been stopped and searched unlawfully, as the Home Office has revealed (Townsend, 2010; Hand, Rishiraj, 2010). In addition it should be pointed out that 'police are not only suspicious of the general public, they also approach new occupational members with suspicion' (Paoline, 2003: 202).

As MacInnes observes, police officers frequently express their sense of isolation from the public as a whole, regardless of race, beliefs, or national origins (in Skolnick, 2009). Several scholars have noted that police show an unusually high degree of occupational solidarity. It is assumed that issues like danger, authoritative pressure, specific legislative powers, and public indifference add to police solidarity. Also, 'the whole civilian world watches the policeman', so at the end of the day officers are limited to the company of other officers (Skolnick, 2009: 583). The need to reach targets and work efficiently highlights the importance of teamwork, which, in turn, contributes to the professional solidarity. As Skolnick (2009) has concluded, the combination of danger and authority should never be permitted to coexist for the sake of the rule of law.

The phenomenon of cop culture exists within a specific social context. Hereby highly problematic issues, such as racism, nationalism, different forms of discrimination and prejudices do not exceptionally occur in police working environment. Police culture, along with its possible positive and functional aspects, unfolds deeper social ills. New forms and tendencies of racism can be detected within society at all its levels, especially after the tragic events of 11 September 2001 in the US, and terror attacks in July 2005 in the UK. Governmental responses to criminal acts on a vast scale not only point to states' powers and potential to amend or enact new legislation, but also to the prominent implications on public views (Alston et al, 2008; Holloway, 2008). Blurring war and crime tools on international level also has continuing consequences on national policing perceptions and practices. Counter-terrorism practices were followed by increased suspicion towards Muslim individuals and towards whole communities.

Reiner (2010) critically evaluates Skolnick's accounts on police working personality, which was defined as a socially generated culture. 'Skolnick's portrait ... failed to draw out the political dimensions of police culture, which reflects and perpetuates the power differences within the social structure' (Reiner, 2010: 118). Furthermore, Reiner writes that 'police officer's experience external political pressure for 'results', more or less so at different times according to particular moral panics or trends in crime statistics' (2010: 119). On the other hand, as it is suggested by Manning, 'public expectations of the police are themselves inflated by police propaganda about their capacities as professional crime-fighters' (in Reiner, 2010: 119). The ambiguity of the police role in the contemporary British society could be seen as one of the difficulties that police face; as an aspect which enforces the negative elements of police culture. Additionally, pressure and ambiguity tend to increase, as it is generated by governmental politics and influenced by security policies in ever changing risk society.

Research into the cop culture observed a motif of a sense of mission, which represents policing as a way of life with a worthwhile purpose; a moral imperative, rather than a job. The purpose includes the preservation of a valued way of life and the protection of the weak (Reiner, 2010). Very often the action-centred, adrenalin producing and macho aspects of policing are highlighted, whereas in reality, points out Reiner (2010), everyday policing is often boring, messy, petty, trivial, and venal. Nonetheless, it is difficult to diffuse police self-perception as "the thin blue line', performing an essential role in safeguarding social order' (Reiner, 2010: 120). In addition, officers are described as cynical, although it might be interpreted as specific response to their working reality. The 'us' and 'them' perspective is one of the notorious aspects of police culture.

As it was observed by Reiner, 'the police perspective on social divisions in the population clearly reflects the structure of power' (2010: 122). Considering the potential danger that citizens may present, police classify them into categories. Internalized mission of war against evil and tendency to categorize citizens reveals another dangerous aspect: 'the police believe themselves to be good judges of moral character, and able to spot who is guilty' (Westmarland, 2008: 256). Presumable consequences of this precarious belief are illustrated by miscarriages of justice. Adverse aspects of police cultures might be traced in historically high profile cases: the Birmingham Six, Ms Judith Ward, the Guildford Four, the Cardiff Three are just a few miscarriages of justice to remember (Ashworth, 1998). As pointed out by Sanders, 'cases are a product of police work, and so the absence of a case is also a police product (1995: 796). Although in a different context, the handling of the investigation of the murder of Stephen Lawrence revealed police unprofessionalism, racial prejudices and gaps in legislation even after the major reforms.

It has been observed that police officers tend to be politically and morally conservative (Reiner, 2010). This characteristic might be explained by the nature of police job. It has been found by psychological research that police job attracts conservative and authoritarian personalities; hence professional training has only temporary effects. Signs of changes are captured in the last quarter of a century, yet, writes Reiner (2010), homophobia remains in police culture, even if it is expressed more covertly. Conservative views paradoxically coexist with frequent emphasis of machismo and its ethos of alcoholic and sexual indulgences. Female police officers experience continuous discrimination. Intense pressure on women from their male colleagues to 'prove themselves' leads to a paradoxical adaptation of the characteristics from the dominant male culture. Furthermore, 'comparable perspectives on being 'a bobby'' are shared between opposing standpoints of minority and majority groups within police (Loftus, 2008: 772). Sexist cultures and practices have a potential to jeopardise the delivery of justice in society – for these reasons some offences might be simply ignored. According to Loftus (2008), police culture has a considerable impact over the internal organizational character and relations between officers. After the Macpherson report (1999) demands for greater diversity in British police forces have increased. Despite that, resentment towards the institutionalization of diversity is demonstrated by particularly white, heterosexual, male officers. Following Loftus (2008), it could be emphasized that change of mentality should go hand in hand with legal reforms and changes in policy, recruitment and training, or else imperious cop culture with all its attributes will continue to persist.

Police racial prejudice still remains a topical issue. Despite social and legal changes, biased, hostile, and discriminative attitudes towards black individuals and other ethnic minorities are still evident. Since the Scarman Report (1981), the Macpherson

Report and later reforms, a greater emphasis was placed on multiculturalism in training and the official force ethos. Nonetheless, individuals from ethnic minority groups are still underrepresented in forces and overrepresented in criminal records. Furthermore, points out Reiner, 'police racial prejudice is in part a reflection of general societal prejudice' (2010: 130). However, argues Reiner (2010), it cannot be assumed that police prejudice translates into behaviour expressing it. Another element of police culture is highly pragmatic, anti-theoretical, down-to-earth perspective (Reiner, 2010). It is noted that training innovations have been made to encourage reflective and analytical skills in police. A research-based approach became mandatory with the legislative requirements to evaluate crime patterns and the effectiveness of crime reduction strategies on local levels (Reiner, 2010). But, since crime became an increasingly politicized issue, political pressures to demonstrate quick crime control results might undermine the training reforms and reinforce the traditional pragmatic stances.

Since 1997 there has been an acceleration of criminal legislation, which expands police powers. However, in 1998 Human Rights were incorporated into English domestic law; in the 2002 Police Reform Act established the Independent Police Complaints Commission (IPCC) responsible for investigating serious allegations against the police (Reiner, 2010). In respect to the IPCC, higher level of scrutiny could be suggested in the process of appointing members of its operational body. Furthermore, the independence of the latter institution is highly questionable. In the context of police powers and accountability, the tragic case of Jean Charles de Menezes in 2005 could serve as a sound example. This death also points to the issues of surveillance and its intersection with human rights, civil liberties, and due process of law.

As Reiner (2010) points out, the police are seen as primarily concerned with preventing and detecting crime. 'The historical and sociological evidence indicate that crime-fighting has never been, and cannot be the prime activity of the police, despite the mythology of media images, cop culture, and ... government policy' (Reiner, 2010: 208). The core mandate of policing is order maintenance. Given this, debates on police powers can be seen in a different spotlight. It has been argued that 'police culture is central to understanding or interpreting the use of police discretion' (Westmarland, 2008: 255). Police decisions may lead to criminalization and stigmatization of individuals or even whole groups of population. The freedom and power to use discretion provides regular opportunities for police officers to engage in corrupt behaviour. Michael Banton (1964) was one of the first scholars to raise concerns on prejudice and discrimination within the framework of power and discretion in the police role (in Westmarland, 2008).

'The plethora of powers available to the police allows them to use intrusion and coercive force which infringes the rights of citizens, such as privacy, personal liberty and freedom of association in a variety of situations in ways that would be 'exceptional, exceptionable or downright illegal' if undertaken by anyone else' (Bowling, Phillips, 2007: 938; Waddington in *ibid.*). This explanation therefore unfolds the importance of transformations in police attitudes and traditional culture(s). In the ideal world police should use their legally defined and justified powers only in the most professional manner. 'The power to stop and search is an investigative power used for the purposes of crime detection or prevention in relation to an individual suspected of a specific offence at a specific time' (Bowling, Phillips, 2007: 938). Despite the legal definitions, in practice these powers sometimes are used for different reasons, not excluding the purposes of general social control. Hence the practical implementation of police culture characteristics might be detected. Moreover, it has been observed that 'the concept of reasonable suspicion is interpreted widely by police officers in practice and that these are marked differences in interpretation within and between police forces' (Bowling, Phillips, 2007: 938). So, the factors or variables that contribute to those professional interpretations could become the issues of focus for the scholars and practitioners.

Waddington (in Westmarland, 2008) represents a different standpoint by calling the focus on police cultures irrelevant for understanding the police. Waddington (*Ibid.*) argues that racist and sexist attitudes are just a part of verbal tradition. Canteen culture is seen as a functional element, which helps to pass on knowledge and strengthens bonds among officers. In response to that it could be argued that racism or any other discriminatory attitudes could hardly be interpreted as positive; or that it does not have an impact on officers' daily decisions and practices. Chan (1996) criticises the existing negative formulation of police culture and suggests a re-conceptualization of the concept. Chan (*Ibid.*) highlights its positive aspects: informal knowledge, for instance, may provide officers with a number of accounts to legitimate their actions. One of the major criticisms is towards a perception of police officers as passive objects, who intercept all the cultural influences. Officers are free (at least to some level) either to accommodate or resist occupational influences and make their personal choices. 'The interpretative and active role of officers in structuring their understanding of the organization and its environment' should be recognized (Chan, 1996: 112).

In summary, therefore, some common aspects of police culture are acknowledged throughout the academic literature: a sense of mission, suspicion, isolation and solidarity, conservatism, machismo, pragmatism, and racial prejudice. However, police culture should not be oversimplified and over-generalized, for the phenomenon is a part of complex social and political relations; and individual, functional, and organizational differences should be taken into consideration. Like any other culture, according to Reiner (2010), police culture is embodied in individuals with different potentials for creativity, different personal backgrounds, experiences and views, different structural positions. Nonetheless, Reiner argues that 'the culture of the police depends not on individual attributes but on elements in the police function itself' (2010: 134). Hence it is worth noting that the scope for the real change is often undermined by the social and political constrains. The National Black Police Association (NBPA), British Association for Women in Policing (BAWP), the Lesbian and Gay Police Association (LAGPA) aim to enhance the knowledge and to educate police services on diversity matters; these organisations are established to advocate reforms, and to provide consultations and support (Loftus, 2008). Nevertheless, even in the 'new' context shocking instances occur. For example, in 2003 BBC documentary undercover investigation '*The Secret Policeman*' exposed outrageous displays of racist behaviour amongst new recruits' (Loftus, 2008: 758). Despite certain qualitative social changes, research show that racist beliefs, xenophobic attitudes and racial prejudices remain widespread in British society (Bowling, Phillips, 2007). As Bowling and Phillips (2007) suggest, critical and fundamental look at the regulation of police coercive powers would be beneficial. The police role in liberal democracies is a fundamental source for a common cop culture features, for police have 'to control crime and disorder in unequal, divided societies while adhering to principles of the rule of law' (Reiner, 2010: 137). Police officers face similar problems and pressures. This specific role in society, although with variations and changes within time and space, continuously generates a typical cultural pattern. Traditional policing landscape is undergoing transformations: the numbers and roles of civilian personnel within the police are expanding. The concept of cop culture is not stagnant and monolithic; and changes are inevitable: police face new qualitative shifts, new problems and challenges.

Bibliography:

Ashworth, A. (2nd Ed., 1998) *The Criminal Process: An Evaluative Study*, Oxford and New York: Oxford University Press

Alston, P. *et al* (3rd Ed., 2008) *International Human Rights in Context: Law, Politics, Morals*, Oxford: Oxford University Press

Bowling, B., Phillips, C. (2007) 'Disproportionate and Discriminatory: Reviewing the Evidence on Police Stop and Search', *The Modern Law Review*, 70 (6), p. 936

Chan, J. (1996) 'Changing Police Culture', *British Journal of Criminology*, 36 (1), p. 109

Hand, T., Rishiraj, A.S. (2010) 'Stops and Searches' in Povey, D. (Ed.) *Police Powers and Procedures, England and Wales 2008/09*, from http://rds.homeoffice.gov.uk/rds/pdfs10/hosb0610.pdf (Accessed: 27/11/2010)

Holloway, D. (2008) *9/11 and the War on Terror*, Edinburgh: Edinburgh University Press Ltd

Loftus, B. (2008) 'Dominant Culture Interrupted: Recognition, Resentment and the Politics of Change in an English Police Force', *British Journal of Criminology*, 48 (6), p. 756

Paoline, E.A. (2003) 'Taking Stock: Toward a Richer Understanding of Police Culture', *Journal of Criminal Justice*, 31, p. 199

Reiner, R. (4th Ed., 2010) *The Politics of the Police*, Oxford: Oxford University Press

Sanders, A. (1995) 'From Suspect to Trial', in Maguire, M., Morgan, R., Reiner, R. (Eds) *The Oxford Handbook of Criminology*, Oxford: Clarendon Press

Skolnick, J.H. (2009) 'A Sketch of the Policeman's 'Working Personality'', in Newburn, T. (Ed.) *Key Readings in Criminology*, Cullompton: Willan Publishing

Townsend, M (2010) 'Black People are 26 Times More Likely than Whites to Face Stop and Search', from http://www.guardian.co.uk/uk/2010/oct/17/stop-and-search-race-figures (Accessed: 27/11/2010)

Westmarland, L. (2nd Ed., 2008) 'Police Cultures', in Newburn, T. (Ed.) *Handbook of Policing*, Cullompton: Willan Publishing